Recipes created, gathered, altered, adjusted by:

Jelena Perisic

Photos styled, taken and edited by:

Suzy Ellis

It all started in Paris...

- as expected, when I first tried macarons. The balance between the sour raspberry filling and the sweet macaron shells was pure perfection! At that moment the idea that I would one day become a patisserie chef didn't even cross my mind. I was an air hostess and very happy to be travelling and exploring delights that other people baked.

- Fast forward 8 years, I was in desperate need of a change and at the time when one starts making lifetime plans, I was offered a macaron course in London. It was a revelation! I could actually do this and I loved it. It was only two years later that I decided to start my own business, knowing it was going to be very challenging, but at the same time very rewarding too.

- As my business grew, so did my knowledge of French patisserie. I explored this new world that had up until then seemed unapproachable. I'll tell you a secret... It is not! I am self-taught and I have had some amazing reviews from many lovely customers and some incredible patisserie chefs. So my very first advice to you all is, follow the recipe, explore and if you fail, try again and mostly, have fun!

Sweet love, from Jelena

Contents:

Macarons

Patisserie

Macaron Shells

The Italian Meringue Method

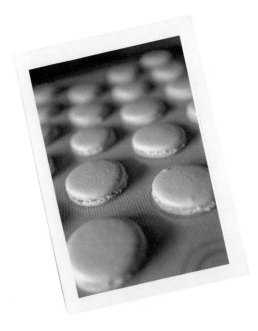

Ingredients:

(makes 60 shells)

150 g icing sugar
135 g ground almonds
50 g egg white
120 g caster sugar
30 ml water
50 g egg white

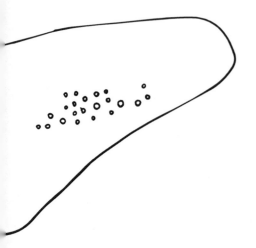

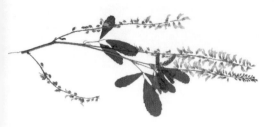

Method:

Pulse blend the icing sugar and ground almonds together, then sieve into a large bowl.

Add 50g of egg white and turn into a smooth paste, using a hand mixer. Cover with cling film, to touch (not allowing any air or moisture in between the cling film ant the mixture).

In a small pan, mix the caster sugar and water. Using a temperature probe, wait until the temperature reaches 115°C. Whisk the 50g of egg white to a medium-stiff peak. When the sugar is at 119°C, start adding it slowly to your egg whites, while continuously mixing, using your hand mixer. Once all the sugar syrup is in, continue mixing until your mix is barely warm to touch.

...Remember how I said if you fail, try again. This might be the time you need to follow that advice! Italian meringue is notoriously difficult to make and please do not give up if you fail the first time (or two). Fun fact: When I went to a macaron course in Paris, with one of the most famous cooking schools, the instructor failed in making his meringue and had to remake one!

So be patient with yourself and give it another go. Here are a few tips that will help get it right:

Meringue Tips:

- Your egg whites need to be at room temperature

- Make sure your bowl is clean and dry, the worst enemies of a meringue are fat and water!

- Whisk your eggs in the same direction
(not sure this one is a thing, but my mum said so!)

- For the Italian meringue, make sure the probe doesn't touch the bottom of the pan and once the syrup is at temperature, double check by moving the probe gently around the syrup.

Add a third of your Italian meringue to your paste and use a hand mixer to fold it in gently (not longer than 2 minutes). The rest of the meringue needs to be added in two stages and folded in using a spatula. You will know that your mixture is ready once you are able to lift it up with your spatula and it forms a ribbon falling back into the bowl. Try to write the number 8 with it and if the ribbon doesn't break, it is perfect!

Pipe on trays, covered with silicon mats or parchment paper, using a Wilton 12 size piping tip. Then leave the macarons to dry for a minimum of 30 minutes. Preheat your oven to 140°C. Once the shells have formed a thin film on the surface, allowing you to touch them without affecting the structure, they are ready to be baked.

Bake for 10 minutes, then turn your tray and bake for 5 more minutes. Once out, leave your macaron shells on the tray for 10-15 minutes. Remove the shells from the silicon mat, or parchment and leave them to cool, before filling.

Macaron Shells - Again

The French Meringue Method

I have to be honest with you here. This is not the recipe I often use. I like the Italian meringue recipe better, as I find it much more forgiving. However I understand that some people might not have a temperature probe, others might want to bake with their children and feel like sugar syrup is too dangerous (and I agree), or they have simply been really unlucky with their Italian meringue and want to try something else... All very valid reasons, that explain why I have decided to include this recipe in the book!

Ingredients:

(makes 60 shells)

180 g icing sugar
100 g ground almonds
90 g egg white
20 g caster sugar

Method:

Pulse blend the icing sugar and ground almonds together, then sieve into a large bowl.

In a separate bowl, whisk the egg whites, slowly adding the caster sugar. Once you have obtained a stiff peak, stop whisking and add in the ground almonds and icing sugar. Using the "macaronage" technique, fold in the egg whites, making sure to take all the mixture from the sides and the bottom of the bowl.

Once the mixture is smooth enough that you can lift up your spatula and form a ribbon with it, it is ready to be piped.

Making sure to leave enough space between each macaron, pipe them onto a silicone mat. Once finished, leave them to dry for at least 30 minutes, Then bake for 13-15 minutes, in a pre-heated oven, at 115°C.

Ingredients:

120 ml semi-skimmed milk

1 medium egg

35g caster sugar

15g plain flour

15g corn flour

1 vanilla pod/1 tsp of vanilla paste

70g unsalted butter

Vanilla macarons

Method:

Cut your vanilla pod into two (length ways) and scrape out the inside using a knife. Pour your milk into a pan, adding the vanilla seeds along with the two pieces of your vanilla pod. Add half of your sugar, making sure to stir the milk regularly.

Once the milk starts to simmer, mix the egg yolk and sugar in a large bowl, using a whisk. After a couple of minutes, add the flour and corn flour and whisk again. As soon as the milk starts to boil, remove the vanilla pods, pour the milk onto the mix, whisk and then move back into the pan and simmer while continuously whisking, until the mixture thickens. Remove from the hob, put into a different dish, cover to touch with cling film and leave to cool in the fridge. Once completely cold you can add it to the previously whisked, softened butter, one spoonful at the time.

Coconut macarons

Replace 20g of ground almonds with 20g of desiccated coconut before blending it with the icing sugar.
You can also decorate your macarons with some desiccated coconut after piping them, in order to give that extra texture to them.

As for the coconut filling, please refer to our American buttercream filling (page 27) – add a tbsp of coconut milk and 30g of desiccated coconut while whisking continuously with a hand mixer. Once ready, you can use this filling straight onto your macarons.

For an extra fresh and summery taste, replace the coconut milk with pineapple juice (make sure it's at room temperature) and enjoy the Pina Colada flavoured macarons!

Chocolate macarons

Ingredients:

40g dark cocoa powder, sieved

100 Dark chocolate (70%)

110g Double cream

When following our macaron shell recipe, replace 40g of icing sugar with 40g of dark cocoa powder. However, if you are making different colours at the same time and you just need a couple of chocolate ones, it is safe to just use a little cocoa powder instead of food colouring.

Chocolate ganache

<u>Microwave method</u> : Break the chocolate into small pieces (or use chocolate chips) and mix them with the cream, in a bowl. Microwave for 30 seconds, then stir well and microwave again for 15 seconds, then stir again, until smooth. Cover and leave to cool in the fridge.

<u>Pan method</u> : Break the chocolate, then put it into a bowl and your cream into a pan. Bring the cream to boil and then pour it onto the chocolate. Leave without stirring for 2 minutes. Once the chocolate has melted stir the mix. Cover and leave to cool in the fridge.

Ingredients:

2 Lemons (unwaxed)

75g caster sugar

7g corn flour

Half a sachet of Agar agar

40g unsalted butter

Lemon filling

Method:

In a small saucepan, mix the lemon zest, lemon juice, caster sugar and corn flour and bring to boil.
Once the mixture has thickened, add Agar agar, mix for a minute and remove from the hob, as it will thicken quickly. Move into a sealed container and leave it to cool down to room temperature (approximately for 30mins).

Beat your slightly melted butter (you will need to leave this at room temperature for a couple of hours before using it). Then add the lemon curd one spoonful at the time and keep whisking. Once your lemon filling is ready, it is better to put it in the fridge for 15-20mins before using it.

You can also use the lemon curd as a dairy-free filling, however the shelf life of your macarons will be shorter.

Raspberry filling

Method:

In a medium saucepan, place the fresh raspberries, then the sugar. Stir so that there is no dry sugar left (to avoid it starting to caramelise). Place on medium heat for 15mins, while stirring regularly. Note that the filling will become much thicker when completely cooled, so do stop the cooking process as soon as you get to a spreadable, jam like consistency.

You can use this as a lovely, home-made raspberry jam, for your scones, cakes, or simply on a slice of toast! Just stop the cooking at 10mins, rather than 15.

Ingredients:

200g fresh raspberries

200g caster sugar

This is what the French call "tant pour tant", the same amount of different ingredients.

Salted caramel filling

Ingredients:

40g Double cream
35g Caster sugar
50g Unsalted butter
Vanilla extract

Method:

Place the sugar and 1 tbsp of water in a pan, over high heat and bring to boil, making sure not to stir at all. In a separate pan, put a drop of vanilla extract into the cream and put on medium heat. Once the sugar starts to turn bright amber colour, take off the heat, add the vanilla cream and stir with a spatula (be very careful not to burn yourself, as the mixture will bubble). Pour the mixture in an airtight container, sprinkle a tsp of salt on top and leave to cool down to room temperature. Beat the butter with a hand mixer, add in the caramel and mix for another 2mins.

After Eight filling

Ingredients:

40g dark chocolate
60g After Eight chocolate
90g double cream

Microwave method:

Mix both chocolates and the cream in a bowl. Microwave for 30 seconds, then stir well and microwave again for 15 seconds, then stir again, until smooth. Cover and leave to cool in the fridge.

Saucepan method:

Put both of your chocolates into a bowl and your cream into a pan. Bring the cream to boil and then pour it onto the chocolate. Leave without stirring for 2 minutes. Once the chocolate has melted stir the mix. Cover and leave to cool in the fridge.

Passion Fruit & White Chocolate filling

Ingredients:

2 Passion Fruits
100g White Chocolate

Method:

If you aren't using chocolate chips, make sure to break the chocolate into quite small pieces, for this recipe.

Slice open both passion fruits and spoon out the pulp into a bowl. Add in your white chocolate chips and stir.

Place into a microwave for 30sec, leave for a minute, then stir to combine. Cool in the fridge for 30mins before use.

Chocolate Orange filling

Ingredients:

40g Dark chocolate
60g Chocolate orange
110g Double cream
Orange zest from 1 orange

Microwave method:

Mix both chocolates and the cream in a bowl. Microwave for 30 seconds, then stir well and microwave again for 15 seconds, add in the orange zest, then stir again, until smooth. Cover and leave to cool in the fridge.

Saucepan method:

Put both of your chocolates into a bowl and your cream into a pan. Bring the cream to boil and then pour it onto the chocolate. Leave without stirring for 2 minutes. Once the chocolate has melted, add in the orange zest and stir the mix.
Cover and leave to cool in the fridge.

Bounty macarons

Ingredients:

100g Coconut buttercream
(see page 13)
50g Dark chocolate

Melt your dark chocolate in a saucepan, over a bain-marie, stirring regularly, until you get to 31°C. Remove from heat and place in a bowl. Fill your white macaron shells with the coconut buttercream, then cover both sides with melted chocolate.

If you are making a large number of macarons and melting more dark chocolate, I'm afraid you will need to temper it! For this, just melt 2/3 of your chocolate, then keep adding the rest slowly, until you reach 31°C.

American Buttercream

American buttercream is a good alternative to the French buttercream filling, especially for the British audience, who don't mind a slightly sweeter taste. It is also great to use for decorative macarons, as you can easily colour it, using colour gel, without altering the consistency of your buttercream. Your macarons will then be a perfect addition to any cake and will be much more stable to transport and leave out, at room temperature.

Ingredients:

50g soft unsalted butter
100g icing sugar, sieved
1tbsp of any flavoured liquid
you wish to flavour your buttercream with
(examples to follow)

Method:

Beat the soft butter, using a hand mixer, until completely smooth. Add a third of the icing sugar and keep whisking. Then add the second third of the icing sugar, while continuously mixing. Finally add the last third of the icing sugar and whisk until white and smooth. You can now add the liquid with which you wish to flavour your buttercream. Mix for a couple of minutes and your icing will be ready to use.

Once piped onto your macarons, store them in the fridge, for at least 30mins before serving. In the same way, you will ideally need to get your macarons out of the fridge 30mins before serving them, to allow the American buttercream to soften a little.

Make sure that the liquid you are adding is at room temperature, otherwise there is a risk of your icing splitting.

Vanilla filling

Preferably using vanilla paste, 1 tsp. For this, you will also need to add a tsp of warm water, in order to soften the buttercream. This is a great alternative to our vanilla macaron recipe, as it can be left out of the fridge for much longer!

Earl Grey filling

Infuse a cup of milk with 2 Earl Grey tea bags the night before. Use 1tbsp of room temperature Earl Grey infused milk to flavour your buttercream.

Chai Tea is another lovely tea to use this way!

Pistachio filling

Ingredients:

50g pistachios
1 tsp olive oil
100g american buttercream

Method:

Start by roasting the pistachios in a frying pan, with 1tsp of olive oil. Once nicely golden, remove from heat and leave to cool. Using a food processor, ground the pistachios, as finely as possible. Add them to your buttercream, mix well and your filling will be ready to use.

Peanut butter & Oreo filling

Split the Oreo biscuits into two and remove the icing.
Break into small chunks (you can place it into a small
plastic bag and use a rolling pin to do this. I simply do it
by hand), then add to your buttercream. Add a tbsp (or
two) of peanut butter to the buttercream, then mix it all
together until well combined.

Ingredients:

2 Oreos

1 tbsp of smooth Peanut butter

100g of american buttercream

Prosecco filling

Simply add 1tbsp of Prosecco to 50g of your
buttercream, whisk for 2 mins and enjoy!
(Make sure your Prosecco is at room temperature)

Baileys filling

Simply add 1tbsp of Baileys to 50g of your buttercream, whisk for 2 mins and enjoy!

For each of these flavourings, you can add more than 1 tbsp of liquid, for a stronger taste, to your personal liking. However, be careful not to add too much, as it will result in your buttercream splitting.

Coffee extract

Ingredient:

100g caster sugar

70g espresso

American
buttercream

Start by making a dry caramel. Put 1/3 of the caster sugar into a pan (I tend to use a frying pan, as the bottom is thinner) and cook at medium to high heat until it starts melting and changing colour. Progressively add the remaining sugar, making sure that the heat is evenly spread. Note that this caramel can be stirred, if needed. Once your caramel is a nice brown colour (darker than our salted caramel recipe, please refer to the photo), slowly add the hot espresso while stirring continuously. Cook for another two minutes, in order for the mixture to thicken slightly. Pour and reserve into a glass jar, where you can keep it, sealed and stored in a fridge, for up to 6 weeks.

Use this to flavour your creme pat' for some delicious coffee eclairs!

Add 2tsp of our coffee extract to the 100g of American buttercream while whisking with a hand mixer, for a delicious coffee filling! If you wish to have a stronger taste, feel free to add some more, as this extract won't really affect the texture of the buttercream.

Crème pâtissière

The must-know of French patisserie!
As you go through the second part of this book,
you will quickly realise how useful this recipe is.
So, get ready to come back to this page... a lot! .

Ingredients:

1L semi-skimmed milk

250g caster sugar

100g egg yolks

40g plain flour

40g corn flour

1 tsp vanilla paste

Pour the milk, vanilla paste and half of the sugar into a saucepan and place on a hob, at medium to high heat, stirring regularly. Once the milk starts to simmer, whisk the egg yolk and sugar together in a large bowl, then add the flour and cornflour and whisk again. Pour the boiling milk onto the egg yolk mixture, then pour everything back into the saucepan and leave to reduce, for about 2 to 3 minutes, whilst stirring continuously. Remove from heat, pour into a bowl, cover with cling film to touch and place in the fridge. Give your crème pât' a quick whisk before using it.

For a chocolate crème pâtissière, do not use vanilla paste. Instead add 50g of dark chocolate before putting your creme pat' back onto the hub.

Fondant:

Place the water, then sugar into a saucepan and heat up to 114 degrees Celsius. Remove from heat and pour straight into a bowl and start whisking using a hand mixer. Keep mixing for about 5 minutes, or until the fondant becomes so thick that it starts to separate into pieces.

Ingredients:

450g caster sugar

150g water

Store the fondant in a sealed container, for up to 3 weeks. Every time you need to use it, add a little water and bring it to 37C. You can also use this fondant for your chocolate pastries, adding a little cocoa powder to it when getting it ready.
If you wish to colour the fondant, it is best to use food colouring gel.

Praline

Ingredients:

200 g whole almonds (with skin)

200g whole hazelnuts (with skin)

260g caster sugar

65g water

Method:

Place the water and sugar in a pan, making sure no sugar is left on the sides of the pan. Using a probe, wait until the temperature reaches 116°C.

Add the nuts and cook at medium to high temperature, while stirring often, until the sugar crystallises. Then turn the heat down and keep cooking until nicely caramelised (medium to dark brown). Pour onto a silicone matt and leave to cool. Once completely cold, blend until you obtain a smooth paste, using a food processor.

Use a table spoon of this paste to flavour your creme pat' or american buttercream!

Mille-Feuille

Ingredients for puff pastry
(makes 4 mille-feuilles)

200g plain flour

50g strong white flour

125g water

5g Salt

200g Unsalted butter

Please refer to pages 38 and 39 for the crème pâtissière and fondant recipe.

Similarly to macarons, many are terrified of even trying to bake a mille-feuille. I believe that with the right recipe and a little patience, anyone can bake anything! So go on, give it a go, I dare you...

Method:

Mix the flour and salt, add 50g of soft butter, cut into cubes, then mix by hand, or using a mixer with a flat beater attachment. Add the water slowly, while mixing continuously. Once the dough   has formed, stop whisking and roll the dough into a ball. Make a cross on the top of the dough, cover with cling film and leave at room temperature for 30mins.

In order to prepare the butter, place it onto a baking parchment, which you then need to fold into a thin rectangle. Tap the butter in order to soften it, then toll into the shape. Once you have obtained the thin rectangular shape, place the butter into the fridge for 30mins.

Pull open each side of your dough, roll it into a cross, then place the butter in the middle. Cover the butter with the dough, making sure the edges are all covered. Roll the dough slightly, cover with cling film, then place in the fridge for 30mins.

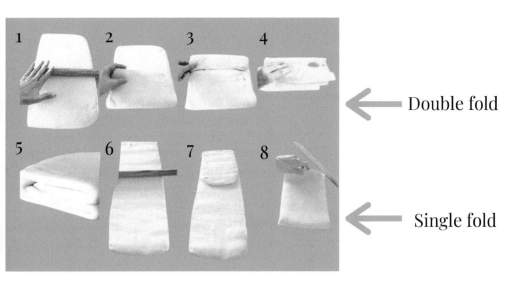

← Double fold

← Single fold

Following the technique shown on the photos above, roll, then fold your dough. Double fold, turn your dough towards the right, roll again, then single fold. Flatten the dough slightly, cover with cling film, then place again into the fridge for 30mins.

At this point, you should make your creme pat', as shown on page 39 and your fondant, following the recipe on page 40.

Repeat the same procedure, starting this time by the single fold. Cling film the dough and place again into the fridge for 30mins.

Roll the pastry, to approximately 3mm thickness, then cut either into three, for a large mille-feuille, or into 12 small pieces, using a template., for individual mille-feuilles.

Cover a baking tray with baking parchment, place your pastry, cover with baking parchment and then with another tray (preferably one that's the same size). Leave the pastry in the fridge for a minimum of 30mins before it's ready to use. Using a small fork make lots of holes in the dough, then sprinkle caster sugar over it.

Bake your puff pastry between two sheets of baking parchment and two trays, at 180°C for 40 mins as a whole sheet, or 35mins if you decide to pre-cut the pastry to the individual parts size.

For the last 5mins of your bake, remove the top tray and parchment sheet, in order to allow the surface of the pastry to caramelise.

While the puff pastry is cooling down, get the creme patissiere out of the fridge, whisk it, using a hand mixer, in order to soften it slightly.

Using a piping bag, cover one sheet of puff pastry entirely with creme pat'. Place another sheet of puff pastry on top and repeat the process. Place the final sheet of pastry on top.

Melt the dark chocolate and place into a paper cone, or a disposable piping bag. Warm the fondant in the microwave, 10 sec at the time, stirring in between. If needed, add a little water to soften. Once the fondant is at 37°C, it's ready to use. Pour it immediately onto the mille-feuille and make the feathered effect using the melted chocolate.

See photo on page 41, for inspiration... But feel free to get creative at this point!

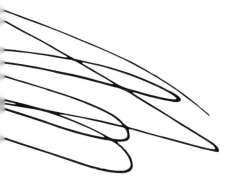

Eclairs

Ingredients for choux pastry:

- 100g water
- 25g milk
- 100g plain flour
- 50g unsalted butter
- a pinch of salt
- 2 medium eggs
- 1 egg yolk (medium)

Please refer to pages 38 and 39 for the crème pâtissière and fondant recipe.

Method:

Preheat your oven at 180°C . Using a small saucepan, bring the water, milk and butter, previously cut into cubes, to boil. Remove from heat, add the flour and salt and mix, using a spatula, until well combined. Place the pan back onto medium heat, for a minute or two, in order to get rid of some moisture. Remove from heat again and place the dough into a bowl. Leave to cool for 3 minutes. Add one egg at a time, making sure the previous one is well combined before adding the second one, Mix with a spatula until combined and the dough on the spatula, makes a "bec d'oiseau" shape, or a bird's beak. Your chou pastry is then ready to be piped.

Bec d'oiseau →

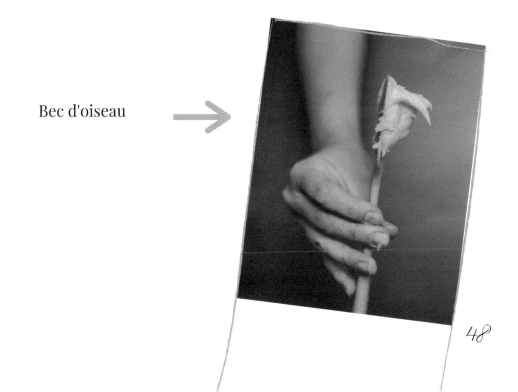

48

Pipe your pastry onto a silicone mat, or baking parchment, forming about 15cm long eclairs. In a cup, mix an egg yolk with a tsp of water. Using a pastry brush, glaze your eclairs. Bake your eclairs for 20-25 minutes at 180°C, then turn the oven down to 115°C, and leave the pastry to dry, for an additional 10 minutes.

Remove your pastry from the oven and leave to cool, before filling with a crème pâtissière of your choice. *(Use our praline and coffee extract recipe to flavour your creme pat')* Then cover the with fondant and place in the fridge for a minimum of 30mins before serving.

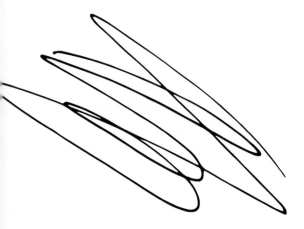

Sweet shortcrust pastry

Ingredients:

250g plain flour
125g melted butter
70g caster sugar
A few drops of vanilla
extract
2 egg yolks (medium)
1tsp of salt

You can make this pastry in a bowl, mixed by hand, or by using a hand mixer. Personally, I use a hand mixer, as I am always worried about overmixing the pastry, if I do it by hand.

First mix the egg yolks with the caster sugar, until white. Add the vanilla extract and salt and whisk again for a few seconds. Then alternate between a third of your flour and half of your butter, starting and finishing with flour.

(So, 1/3 flour, ½ butter, 1/3 flour, ½ butter, 1/3 flour) The amounts used each time don't have to be exact. Once everything is well combined, take your pastry out of the mixer, work it briefly with your hands, film and leave to cool in the fridge for 2 hours.

Once your pastry has cooled down, it should be nice and easy to roll and cut to fit your tin. Fit into your tin nicely, making sure the sides are well pressed against the tin and cutting off any excess pastry at the top. Using a dessert fork (or similar) make holes at the bottom of your pastry, allowing the air and condensation to circulate and making your pastry stay in place. Cook at 170°C for 15minutes, or until slightly golden in colour. Leave it to cool down to room temperature before use.

Fruit Tarts

You can use this pastry to create all sorts of different tarts, but the easiest one by far is the red fruit tart. All you need to add is (lucky guess?...) yes, creme pat'!

Just follow our recipe and make sure both your pastry and creme pat' are properly cooled before you use them. You can then add any red fruit you like, as much as you like, in order to make the perfect summer tart. I use the exact same recipe for my strawberry tarts.

In order for your fruit to be nice and shiny, just follow the recipe below for an easy glaze. However, if you are serving the tart on the same day, you can skip this step.

Bring the same amount of water and caster sugar to boil (in the case of a large tart, I would recommend 50g). Add half a sachet of Agar Agar, stir well and remove from hob. Use a pastry brush to glaze the fruit on your tart and make it look picture perfect!

Lemon Meringue Tart

Ingredients:

Lemon curd:

3 medium eggs

150g caster sugar

3 lemons, squeezed

Zest from 2 of those lemons

45g unsalted butter

Meringue:

2 egg whites (medium egg)

130g caster sugar

40g water

15g lemon juice

Lemon curd:

To make your lemon curd, put all of your ingredients, except for the butter, into a medium size saucepan. Whisk it well, to combine everything, before putting your pan onto medium heat. Keep whisking while the mixture cooks, for about 5 minutes, or until nice and light in colour. At that point you can add the butter, while whisking constantly. Once your butter has melted and integrated into the mixture, your curd is ready! Cover it to touch and wait until it gets to room temperature before pouring it your pastry case.
It should come all the way to the top of the tin. Place the tart into the oven, at 170C for 15mins. Once cooked, leave it to cool, then store in the fridge until ready to be served.

Italian Meringue:

(with a hint of lemon juice)

Put the water and sugar into a small pan and cook until it reaches 115°C, at that point start whisking your egg whites. Once your sugar syrup is at 118-120 degrees pour it onto your egg whites, while whisking them constantly. Once your meringue appears to be stiff, you can add the lemon juice to it. Keep whisking until the side of your bowl is cool to touch. Once your meringue is ready, put it into a piping bag and pipe onto your tart. You can then choose to leave it as it is, or blowtorch the top.

You will most likely have some leftover meringue here, in which case you can also cook it at 100C for 1h30-2hrs. If you prefer your meringue baked, this is also something you can do beforehand and just place your small meringues directly onto your tart.

and fell in love with it.
build the villa as a holiday

Ingredients:

Enriched shortcrust pastry/ Pate sablee

240g plain flour

80g caster sugar

120g unsalted butter

1 medium egg

1/2 tsp baking powder

A pinch of salt

8 Apples
 (3 green apples & 5 golden apples)

1tsp ground cinnamon

½ tsp ground nutmeg

40g caster sugar

20g light brown sugar

50g unsalted butter

1tbsp apricot jam

Apple Tart

In a large bowl, mix all of your dry ingredients (flour, sugar, baking powder, salt). Add soft butter and start mixing by hand, passing it through your fingers in order to create crumbs. You can also use a pastry mixer, for about 2mins. Once your mixture has a nice, crumbly texture, you can add your egg in and work the dough into a ball. Cover with cling film and leave in the fridge for minimum of 3 hours (Ideally you would prepare this pastry the day before).

Method:

Start by making your compote, as it will need to cool down before you use it.

Peel and finely chop 3 green apples and one golden apple. In a pan add a small glass of water, your apples, caster sugar, nutmeg and cinnamon. Cook at medium heat for 15-20mins, stirring the mixture frequently, until the apples are cooked and the mixture reduced. Pour the mixture into a bowl and leave it to cool down to room temperature while getting your apples and pastry ready.

Preheat the oven to 170C. Take your pastry out of the fridge. Peel and slice the remaining apples (as shown on the photo). Put some flour on your worktop and roll the pastry to about 3mm thickness. Grease your tin and dust with flour before putting the pastry, then push down the edges, using your thumbs (on at the bottom and one on the side of the tin) Cut off any excess pastry from the sides of your tin. Pour your compote to fill ¾ of the tin, as you will need some space for the apples. Arrange the apples as shown on the photo, or any way that you like, sprinkle some brown sugar on top, cut your butter into small pieces and add on top of the tart as well. Bake for 30-35 minutes, until golden and caramelised. Warm the apricot jam with a little water then, using a pastry brush, glaze the apples. Your tart is ready to be served!

Crêpes

Ingredients:

3 medium eggs

350ml milk

300g plain flour

A pinch of salt

A pinch of caster sugar

Flavouring (vanilla, lemon zest, orange zest etc.)

Ok, so before I start, I have to confess that I have never measured the ingredients for crepes before writing this book. To me it's always been second nature, as this is the very first thing I ever baked in my life. Please use this as a family recipe that everyone can participate in making and explore all the different flavourings and fillings. My best memories are the "crepe night" ones and hope that you will create some wonderful ones too!

Method:

Start by whisking the eggs, then add a third of the flour. Once the mixture is smooth, with no lumps, you can slowly add a third of the milk, while continuously whisking. Repeat the procedure, adding this time the salt and your flavouring.

Finally, add the last third of flour, whisk until smooth and stop the mixer. Add the last third of milk, while gently stirring with a ladle.

Put a tea spoon of butter in a frying pan, over high heat, wait for a couple of minutes and then pour in one ladle full of crepe mixture, while moving the pan, to spread the mixture around. Cook each side for 2mins, then place your crepe on a plate and cover with foil to keep warm, while baking the rest of your crepes.
Fill your crepes with your favourite fillings and enjoy!

Galettes de Sarrasin

Ingredients:

200ml whole milk

250ml water

5 g sea salt

100 g plain flour

150g buckwheat flour

40 g butter

2 medium eggs

50ml cider

1tsp of ground pepper

Method:

Melt the butter and leave it to cool at a room temperature. Mix both flours together. Separately, mix the eggs, milk, water and cider, then add it to your dry ingredients while whisking at a medium speed. Finally add the cooled butter, the salt and pepper and whisk it all together, until obtaining a smooth texture. Leave the mixture in the fridge for 2 hours before using. Once out, give the mixture a stir and it will be ready to use! Butter your frying pan and cook your galette on each side for about 2 minutes (or until lightly golden). Your galettes will have small holes in them, don't try to fill them, that is perfectly normal. Once all your galettes are ready, prepare your fillings on the side and mix and match as you wish! Put a single galette back on your pan, at medium heat, add your fillings and fold as shown on the photo.

Ideas of fillings to go into your galettes:

-The traditional and the most commonly used filling is egg, ham, gruyere cheese and a dash of ground black pepper. For this, one would normally break the egg in the middle (as this is the ingredient that takes the longest to cook), then add the ham around and the cheese on top.
To add some flavouring to this you can dice some mushrooms and tomatoes, fry them with a seasoning of your choice (Mediterranean spices is what I would normally use) and add that onto your galette before you add the cheese.

-Another popular filling amongst galette lovers is: goat cheese (preferably medium to strong), honey and walnuts. As previously, just put your galette back on your pan, on medium heat, add your fillings, starting with the cheese, fold it nicely, let it all melt and cook until golden, light brown in colour et voila!

-Last, but not least, the slightly more sophisticated filling: salmon, crème fraiche, prawns. To season this, add a dash of lemon to your crème fraiche and season with some fresh chives and some dill.

Croque-Monsieur / Madame

Ingredients:

8 Slices of bread (of your choice)

4 slices of ham

100g grated Gruyere (or Cheddar)

Ingredients for Béchamel sauce:

30g butter

30g plain flour

500ml milk

50g grated Gruyere (or Cheddar)

salt, black pepper &

mustard powder, to season

Method:

Start by making the béchamel sauce... Place the butter in a saucepan and melt, until slightly golden. Add all the flour at once and stir very vigorously, until a smooth, thick paste is obtained. Slowly add the milk, while continuously whisking. Once all the milk is in, make sure there aren't any flour lumps, by occasionally whisking firmly. Add in the grated cheese and cook for another 5mins. Remove from heat, your sauce will then be ready to use.

On a baking tray, place a slice of the bread of your choice. Spread some bechamel sauce on it, then add a slice of ham, then a spoonful of bechamel sauce, followed by the second slice of bread. Repeat the process with all the bread. then spread some more bechamel sauce on the top of all your croque-monsieurs, Cover then with gruyere and place in a pre-heated oven (200°C) for 15-20mins, or until golden. Season to your liking and enjoy!

Transform your Croque-Monsieur into a Croque-Madame simply by adding an egg on top, before cooking. You might need to create a little gruyere nest, in order to keep the egg in place.

Quiche Lorraine

Ingredients:

(shortcrust pastry)

125g unsalted butter, soften

250g plain flour

a pinch of salt

100ml water

(filling)

200g smoked bacon (or 5 slices)

30g red onions

3 medium eggs

400g creme fraiche

150g gruyere cheese

ground pepper, to season

Method:

Start by making your shortcrust dough, as this one will need to be chilled for 1 hour, before being used. You can also make the dough in advance and freeze it.

Put the flour and salt in a large bowl and add the cubes of butter.
Use your fingertips to rub the butter into the flour until you have a mixture that resembles coarse breadcrumbs with no large lumps of butter remaining. Try to work quickly so that it does not become greasy.

Using a table knife, stir while slowly adding the cold water in order to bind the dough together. Gently knead the pastry on a clean work surface until it just comes together. Like for our previous pastries, you don't want to overwork this one. Cover the pastry with cling film and leave in the fridge for a minimum of one hour.

Finely dice the onion and bacon, then fry in a pan, for 5mins. Place the mixture onto some kitchen roll, in order to get rid of the grease. In a medium size bowl, whisk your eggs and creme fraiche, then add in the bacon and onion.

Preheat your oven to 200°C. Roll your pastry onto a tart tin, then add your mixture. Season with ground pepper, grate the cheese on top, then cook for approximately 20mins.

Serve your quiche hot, or cold, with a nice salad and enjoy!

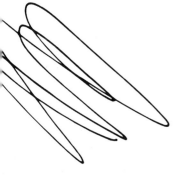

Thank You!

To Suzy, who helped make this project possible by taking these gorgeous photos, but also by inviting me to attend the macaron making course, back in 2015.

To my boys, Gregor & Viktor, for their unconditional love and for our amazing crepe making/ "Greatest Showman" singalong evenings!

To Scott, my partner, my biggest support, from the very beginning and for always being very patient with me taking over the kitchen!

To my family, my mum Marina, for giving me the baking basics. My brother Miki, for teaching me to always be extra careful while baking (as we have ended up with crepe mixture all over the carpet as kids), to both of them and Richard, for their continuous love and support.

To Gill & Chris, for always being supportive, helping at every step of my business and for letting me borrow their kitchen for our photoshoot!

To my beautiful nieces, Stasa & Neda and their mum Sandra, for always inspiring me to be a better mum and bake more with my little ones.

To all of my friends, for their love and support, their words of encouragement and for never letting me give up!

To Graeme, Bonnie & Rory, for letting me borrow Suzy for hours and hours and for the lovely smiles on their faces every time they would eat my macarons.

Last but not least, a huge THANK YOU to all of my customers, for their orders, their reviews, their lovely words, their recommendations and their kindness. I couldn't have done this without you!

Love you all, Jelena